The Moonsnoop

Written by Alison Hawes
Illustrated by Angie Sage

Andrew drew the plans for a moon rocket.
"This is the Moonsnoop," he said to
his sister, Sue.

Sue thought the Moonsnoop looked cool.
"We could make the Moonsnoop today!"
she said.

3

Andrew and Sue looked in the
garden shed for things they could use.

They took an old broom, a boot, a spoon
and a red fuse and glued them to a box.

Andrew thought the Moonsnoop looked good.
"We just need to paint it blue," he said.
"Then we can zoom off to the moon!"

"I will be the pilot of the Moonsnoop,"
Andrew said. "You and Ted can be
the crew."
Sue said, "But I would like to be a
pilot, too!"

Andrew put on his moon boots.
Sue put on her moon jacket and
helmet.

8

Andrew gave the broom a push.
Sue gave the spoon a pull, and off
they flew to the moon!

Whoosh went the Moonsnoop as it flew through the sky.

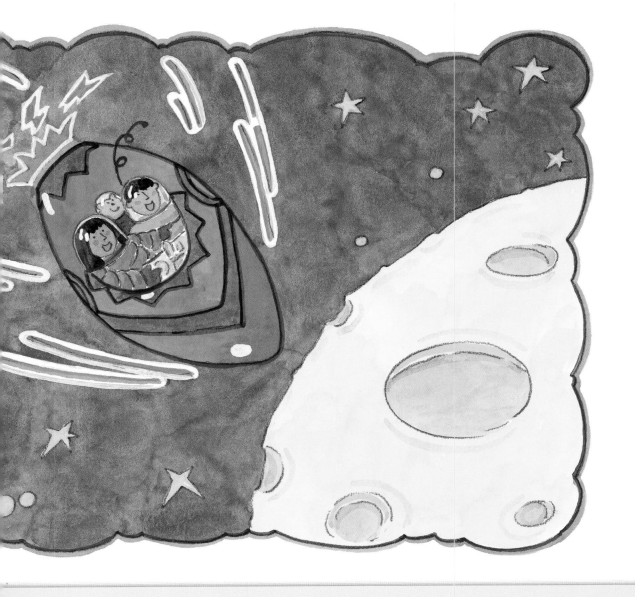

"We will soon be on the moon,"
said Andrew.

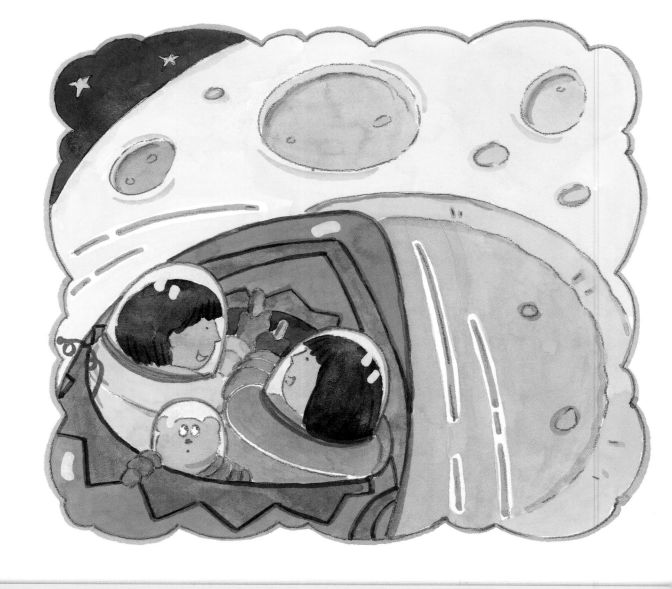

Andrew gave the broom a pull.
Sue gave the spoon a push.

Oops! With a crash, the Moonsnoop
flew onto the moon.

Then Andrew and Sue spotted
some moonbugs looking at them.
The moonbugs went **bleep**!

Sue and Andrew gave the moonbugs some sweets. The moonbugs gave them a blue moon drink!

Then Andrew and Sue said,
"We should go now. Would you like
us to come again?"
"Yes, we would!" said the moonbugs.
"Come back soon!"